CHILDREN'S HOME CARE SERIES

Cleaning

LIFE SKILLS

CHILDREN'S HOME CARE SERIES

Cleaning

HERON BOOKS

Published by
Heron Books, Inc.
20950 SW Rock Creek Road
Sheridan, OR 97378

heronbooks.com

Special thanks to all the teachers and students who
provided feedback instrumental to this edition.

Printed in the USA

31 January 2024

At Heron Books, we think learning should be engaging and fun. It should be hands-on and allow students to move at their own pace.

To facilitate this we have created a learning guide that will help any student progress through this book, chapter by chapter, with confidence and interest.

Get learning guides at
heronbooks.com/learningguides.

For teacher resources,
such as a final exam, email
teacherresources@heronbooks.com.

We would love to hear from you!
Email us at *feedback@heronbooks.com.*

IN THIS BOOK

CHAPTER 1

Sweeping

CHAPTER 1

Sweeping

Sweeping is a way of getting dirt and dust off of some things to make them clean.

Sweeping is done with a broom and a dustpan.

broom   dustpan

The dirt and dust is pushed into a pile using the broom. The dustpan is used to pick up the dust and dirt so it can be thrown away.

Some things you can sweep are floors, sidewalks and stairs.

BROOM AND DUSTPAN—HOW TO USE THEM

A broom is used for sweeping. It is made of straw or some other material tied together and attached to a long stick.

A dustpan is kind of like a shovel with a short handle. You sweep dust and dirt into it so you can throw away the dust and dirt.

broom

dustpan

You hold a broom and move it like this:

You push the broom along the floor or ground. This sweeping movement of the broom is done to move the dirt and dust where you want it to go. To make sure you don't leave any dirt as you sweep along, you need to push down a little on the broom.

The dirt and dust is easiest to pick up if you sweep it into one big pile. When you have all the dirt and dust in one big pile, you hold the dustpan and broom like this:

You move the broom so it pushes the dirt and dust into the dustpan. Then carefully carry the dustpan to a wastebasket and throw away the dust and dirt.

Remember your purpose for sweeping—you want the dirt and dust off the floor or ground.

Move chairs and boxes and other things out of your way as you sweep. Sweep under tables and pianos and things like that. Remember there is dirt and dust *under* things, too!

Sweep your floor every day to keep it clean.

CHAPTER 2

Mopping

CHAPTER 2

Mopping

A **mop** is something made for washing floors. A mop can be a bunch of thick yarn on a long stick or a mop can be a sponge on a long stick.

MOPPING

Mopping is cleaning floors with a mop.

Floors get dirty. It is not always enough to just sweep. About once a week you need to mop your floors. Mopping is done with a mop and hot water that has floor cleaner in it.

GERMS

A **germ** is a tiny, tiny animal or plant so small you can't see one with your eyes. Some germs can cause sickness. Some do no harm. Germs grow fast in dirty places.

Floors can *look* clean but have germs on them. Washing the floor once a week kills a few of the germs and keeps the floor clean so the germs don't grow as fast.

USING A MOP

You hold a mop a bit differently than you hold a broom. Your hands go on a mop like this:

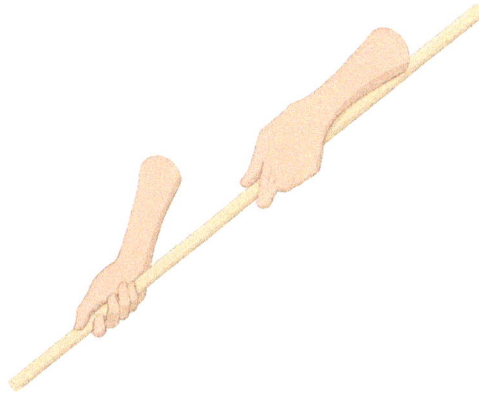

Push and pull the wet mop, back and forth. The dirt comes off the floor onto the mop as you push the mop back and forth along the floor. After you have mopped for a bit, the mop gets a lot of dirt on it. Stick it in the bucket of water to get the dirt off. Then squeeze it and continue mopping.

WET FLOORS

Puddles are something you *don't* want when you are mopping! The mop should only be wet, not dripping. If too much water is used, the floor will dry with spots that still look dirty.

A sponge mop has a metal squeezer on it to squeeze out the water from the mop. This helps to make sure the mop is not too wet. A yarn mop has to be squeezed with your hands or a big squeezer that goes on the bucket.

CHAPTER 3

Cleaning Floors

CHAPTER 3

Cleaning Floors

LIQUID

A **liquid** is something that pours and is wet. Grape juice is a liquid, water is a liquid, milk is a liquid.

FLOOR CLEANER

Floor cleaner helps clean the floor better. You put in the hot water you use to clean the floor. Some floor cleaners are liquid. They usually come in bottles.

Some floor cleaners are powdery soap. They usually come in boxes.

RINSE

Rinse means to remove soap by using clean water. When you wash your body or your hair, you rinse the suds off with clean water.

RINSING FLOORS

If you use sudsy floor cleaner to mop your floor, you will need to rinse the floor with clean water and a clean mop when you are done. This removes the suds left on the floor.

There are some floor cleaners that will need to be rinsed off after mopping even if there are no suds. You should always read the directions on the bottle or box of cleaner, and follow them.

CLEANING A MOP

When you are finished with the mop, you need to clean the dirt and germs from it before you put it away. Here is how you do it:

Fill the sink half full of warm water. Put the mop in the water and let the water soak into the dirty mop. Then squeeze out the water into the sink. Soak the mop and squeeze it several times. The water in the sink will get dirty as you do this.

After you have soaked and squeezed the mop several times, let the dirty water out of the sink. Fill the sink half full of warm water again. Soak and squeeze the mop a few more times. When you can squeeze the mop and the water in the sink doesn't get dirty, then you have a clean mop!

Let the water out of the sink and clean the sink if it is dirty from the dirty water. Put the mop away where it belongs. Stand the mop up with the yarn or sponge part near the ceiling so it dries faster.

CHAPTER 4

Baseboards

CHAPTER 4
Baseboards

A **baseboard** is at the bottom edge of a wall, where the wall meets the floor. A baseboard can be made of wood, plastic or rubber.

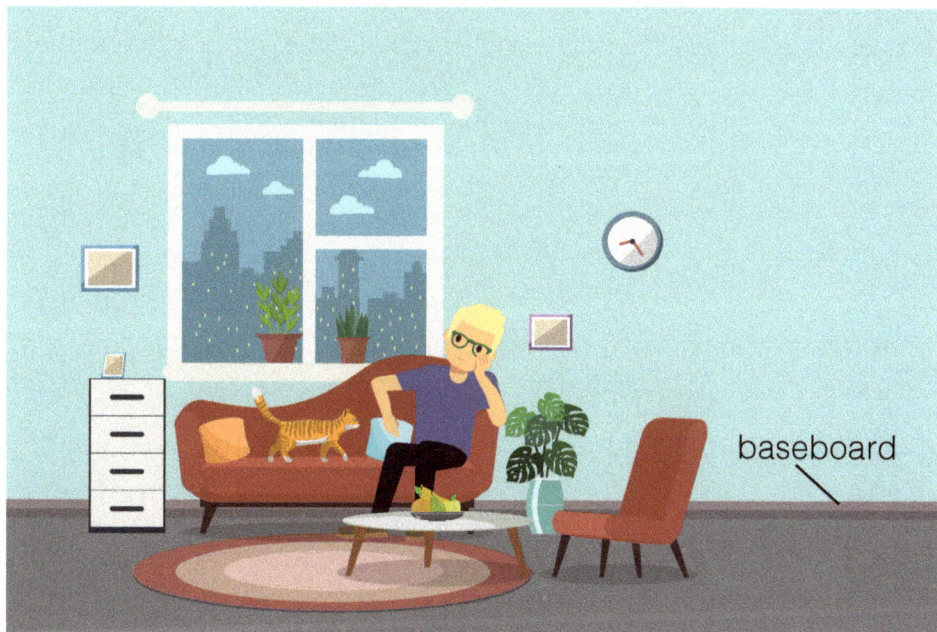

baseboard

A **scrub brush** is a small hand brush used for cleaning.

When cleaning a room, a mop or broom cannot clean the baseboards and the edge of the floor very well. Brooms and mops cannot get into the cracks or clean around things well.

To clean baseboards you need a scrub brush. One piece of the brushing part of a brush is called a **bristle**. You can find a bristle on your toothbrush or hair brush or other brushes.

—————— bristles

The bristles of the brush get the dirt out of the crack between the floor and the baseboard. They also clean the edge of the floor where dirt and water get left from mopping and sweeping.

CLEANING WITH A SCRUB BRUSH

To clean with a scrub brush, use hot water with a floor cleaner, just as you did for mopping the floor. Wet the scrub brush by sticking it in the water. Then scrub the baseboard with the brush until all the dirt comes off. Wipe the baseboard dry with a towel when you are done cleaning it.

CHAPTER 5

Vacuuming

CHAPTER 5

Vacuuming

VACUUM CLEANER

A **vacuum cleaner** is a machine that sucks up dust and dirt and stores it in a bag that is on or in the vacuum cleaner. There are several kinds of vacuum cleaners.

hose

VACUUMING FLOORS

Vacuuming is cleaning a rug or floor with a vacuum cleaner. Vacuuming is really fun and easy to do. Just turn on the vacuum cleaner after plugging it in, and start moving it across the floor! You must move the vacuum cleaner across the floor the right way, though, or it won't get clean. What works best is to go back and forth in lines across the rug or floor as you vacuum, like this:

Just keep going back and forth, not missing any spots.

If there is furniture where you want to vacuum, move it before starting.

VACUUMING OTHER THINGS

A **crevice** is a crack or opening that is not very wide.

crevice

A **tool** is something made to help a person do a job better. A hammer is a tool, a rake is a tool, a brush is a tool!

Vacuum cleaners have things called **attachments**. These are tools that attach to the hose of the vacuum cleaner to clean other things besides floors.

crevice tool   brush tool

There are many different vacuum attachments. Vacuum attachments are used to clean places the big cleaner part of the vacuum can't.

The brush tool is used for furniture and curtains. If you want to vacuum any of these things, just attach your brush tool.

A crevice tool is used to vacuum baseboards and the part of the rug close to the baseboards. It is used to vacuum other cracks and openings that are hard to get to. A crevice tool is very useful!

www.ingramcontent.com/pod-product-compliance
Lightning Source LLC
Chambersburg PA
CBHW041433040426
42450CB00023B/3481